ALASKA INDIAN BASKETRY

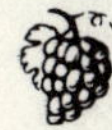

By

LLOYD W. MACDOWELL

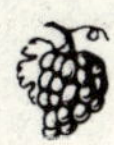

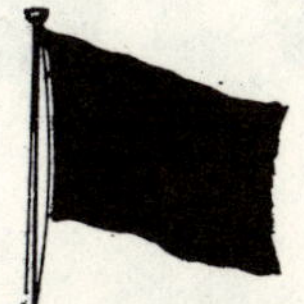

PUBLISHED BY

THE ALASKA STEAMSHIP COMPANY

SEATTLE, WASHINGTON

MDCCCCIV

Facsimile Reprint
1973

The Shorey Book Store
Seattle, Washington

SJS # 21

Sixth Edition

150 Copies
1973

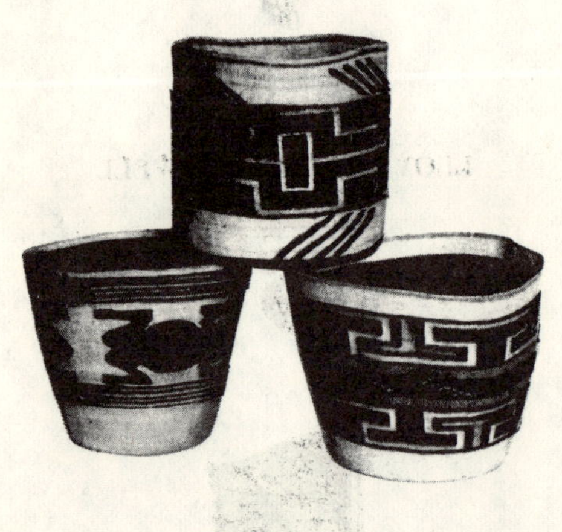

Shorey Publications
Seattle, Washington

NO HOME is complete now-a-days without a neat and artistically arranged Indian basket corner.

The fad of collecting these beautifully woven gems—the handiwork of the North American aborigines—is one which is fast finding favor with those who journey northward.

What a pleasure to wander about in the quaint Indian villages which still have the primitive charm; stop now and then to gaze upon the venerable totem poles or poke your way into the countless huts and igloos in search of the rare and curious relics.

Indian tribes in the North usually select the shores of the mainland for their places of abode. Many have settled on the islands which dot the coast of British Columbia and Southeastern Alaska. Nature especially favored that section of the Pacific and the quiet waters for more than a thousand miles are peppered over with islets and archipelagoes in bewildering profusion.

There the waves spread over the long and rocky island beaches leaving the whip-shaped kelp, mosses and other forms of sea life to dry and wither away while the swells continue in their mad rush to the farther shore where they dash and break against the rugged promontories throwing the silvery spray high into the air.

For a background nature set in place high and stately mountains whose peaks are snow-capped and cloud-hung the year around. Down their sides rush nundreds of narrow and swollen streams booming and roaring on their way to the ocean. Mighty glaciers fill the valleys and at intervals go tumbling into the sea where the sun casts its rays over the jagged bergs forming kaleidoscopic color effects of rare beauty.

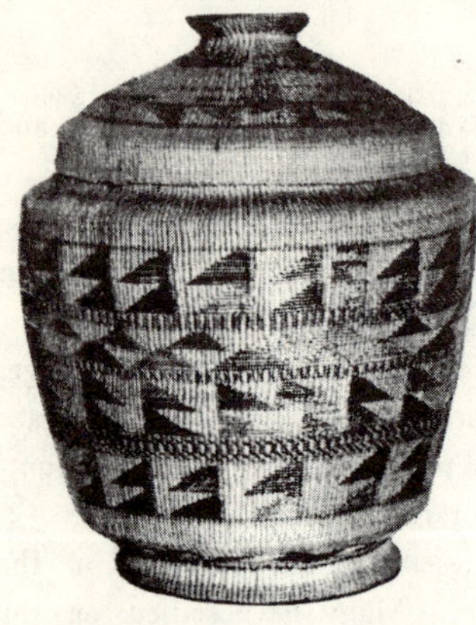

Out in the ocean the wooded islands—some but a mere speck of volcanic origin while others are miles in length—stand like sentinels guarding the entrance to this veritable fairyland. Along the shores of these lonely islands, and along the coast Alaska's natives will be found ready and eager to display their baskets, odd carved totems and fine bead work. To say the least, Alaska basketry is one of the most interesting phases of Indian life and the skillful men and women deserve unstinted credit for weaving the exquisite and highly-colored fabrics which ultimately find their way into thousands of well ordered homes.

THE ALASKA STEAMSHIP COMPANY'S ALASKA FLEET

In addition to its Puget Sound fleet of seventeen steamers The Alaska Steamship Company operates on the Southeastern Alaska Route, between Seattle and Skagway and intermediate Alaska ports, the A1, and popular and reliable steamers

DOLPHIN   *JEFFERSON*
FARALLON   *a n d*   *DIRIGO*

Sailing from Seattle every three to five days for all Southeastern Alaska ports. Their officers are men of known ability and long experience in the navigation of the wonderful "inside passage" to Alaska.

A peculiar little knife-blade fitted into a bone handle is used by the weavers. After the slender fibre has been separated from the root one end is fastened to a stick set firmly in the ground. With a crude copper instrument or mussel-shell it is scraped until it has a fine, glossy or smooth appearance.

This is a long and tedious task, but the weaver cannot commence her work until hundreds of the slender strands have been secured. In each instance the bottom of the basket is first woven. It is held in shape by crossed sticks temporarily sewed to the circle of fabric while the sides or walls are slowly built up. Collectors say that one of the many reasons for the superiority of Yakutat baskets is the fact that weavers use every possible care while engaged in the work of weaving. Each piece of basketry is wrapped in silk or other clean cloth and this invariably follows to completion. Those who have visited the Yakutat villages tell how the women wrap the basket in cloth to prevent dirt from working its way in between the strands and spoiling the effect of the color work. After the basket is finished it remains covered until sold to the tourist or dealer. Many persons who have made the trip to Alaska will recall how the Indians came out to the steamer in their canoes to display their wares and it was a notice- able fact that each basket was neatly wrapped.

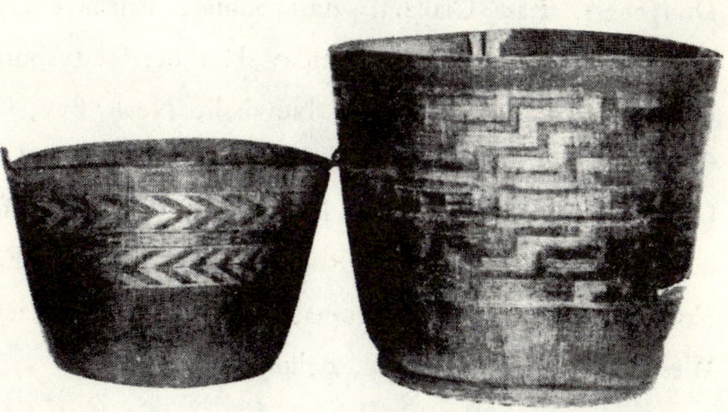

Steamers and Ports of Call

STEAMERS

Dolphin, Dirigo, Farallon, Rosalie, Jefferson, Whatcom, Bellingham, Dode, Athlon, Alice Gertrude, Geo. E. Starr, Fairhaven, Prosper, Utopia, Lydia Thompson, Garland, Inland Flyer, Port Orchard, Samson, Rapid Transit, T. W. Lake.

PORTS OF CALL

SOUTHEASTERN ALASKA ROUTE

Ketchikan, Wrangel, Petersburg, Juneau, Douglas City, Haines, Skagway, Metlakahtla, Hadley, Loring.

PUGET SOUND ROUTES

Anacortes, Argyle, Blaine, Bremerton, Brown's Point, Camano, Charleston, Clinton, Coupeville, Deer Harbor, Diamond Point, Dungeness, East Clallam, East Sound, Fairhaven, Fort Casey, Fort Flagler, Fort Worden, Friday Harbor, Gettysburg, Kingston, LaConner, Langley, Lopez, Newhall, Neah Bay, Oak Harbor, Olga, Orcas, Pleasant Beach, Port Angeles, Port Crescent, Port Gamble, Port Ludlow, Port Madison, Port Townsend, Port Williams, Pysht, Richardson, Roche Harbor, San De Fuca, Seattle, Sidney, Smith's Island, Tacoma, Twin, Utsalady, Victoria, B. C., West Clallam, West Sound, Bellingham.

Modern Indian Basketry

Specific terms for the rich and gaily decorated Indian baskets
have been in use but a very few years. The names Attu and
Yakutat are now exalted above all others. Attu is the name of the
westermost island of the Aleutian chain lying in about 172 degrees
of east longitude and 53 degrees of north latitude, and its location
precludes the growth of wood-bearing plants. The natives of Attu
island had no roots or bark to use in their baskets, like the tribes at
the southern extremity of Alaska, but they did have the fine and
tough grasses. With these the women weavers learned to fashion
fabrics excelling all others in the delicacy of their tissues. Before
the Aleuts came in contact with the whites their baskets were
finished without the use of colors. When they met with the early
traders they obtained bright worsteds and yarns. These they deftly
used in ornamenting the baskets.

Since basketry became popular in America these soft and pliable
baskets of the Aleuts have almost doubled in value. The most
famous of all offered for sale came from Attu island and now that
name is the common one used when reference is made to that dis-
tinctive type of weave and material. The Indian population of
Attu island was never large and it is now claimed by experienced
collectors
that less
than forty
weavers
are left and
the wom-
en confine
their ef-

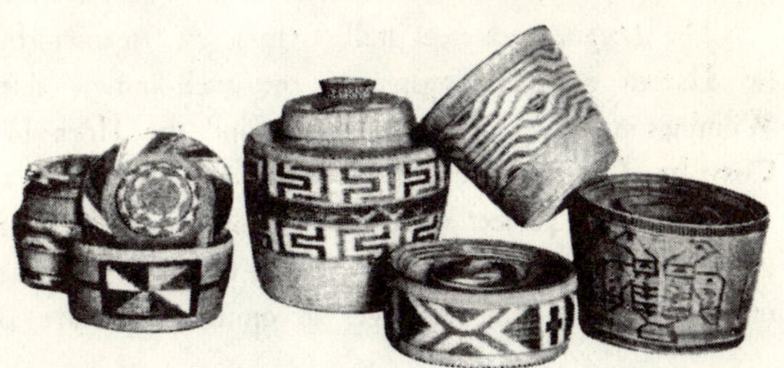

forts to the manufacture of tiny cigarette cases. The Attu baskets bring a big price and range in value from $25 to $150.

Probably the largest basket ever woven was one made a number of years ago and sent to Helen Gould. This young woman heard that the natives of Attu island were in a starving condition and contributed liberally to their needs. The natives desired to show their appreciation and one old woman in the village began the task of constructing a mighty basket. Though nearly blind this aged weaver finished it after months of hard work. This basket is now said to be the masterpiece of the Aleutian race and it is not likely it will ever be duplicated.

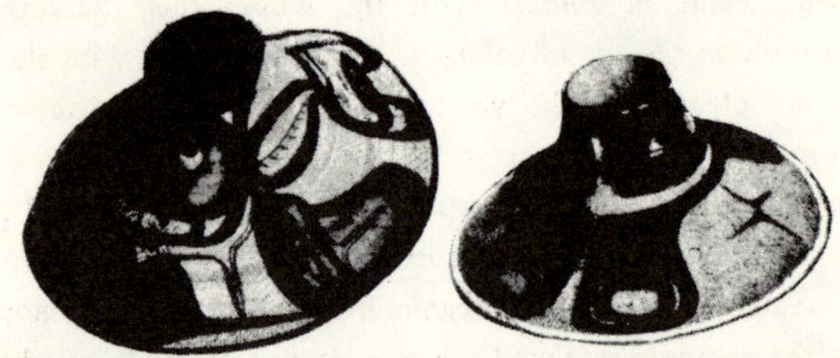

The Alaska Flyers, the *Dolphin* and the *Jefferson*, are two of the most popular, best and fastest boats in the Alaska service.

The *Dolphin* is a steel hull, twin-screw steamer, built in 1892 by Harlan and Hollingsworth, the well-known shipbuilders at Wilmington, Del., and brought around the Horn to the Pacific Coast by The Alaska Steamship Company four years ago. She is 225 feet long, 40 feet wide and is equipped with two sets of high-grade triple expansion engines. She is considered the fastest steamer on the route. Her passenger accommodations are of the very highest order in point of furnishings, convenience of arrangements, etc., and with her unexcelled dining service and speed account for her great popularity.

The *Jefferson* is a new, ocean-going steamer, built by the Company at Tacoma, expressly for the Southeastern Alaska service, the plans being based on years of observation and experience in Alaskan waters. She has a large freight capacity under decks, and enjoys the distinction of being the only steamer running to Alaska that is equipped almost exclusively with large two-berth rooms, which are so much more satisfactory to passengers than three-berth rooms. The social hall and ladies' parlor, and smoking rooms are large and luxuriantly furnished. The cuisine is not surpassed on the Coast. She is a new vessel, launched April 2nd, 1904, 226 feet long; beam 38 feet; depth 25 feet. Speed about 15 knots.

These two splendid vessels, alternating on a ten-day schedule, though really making the round trip of 2000 miles between Seattle and Skagway in 6½ to 8 days, sail from Seattle every fifth day, touching at the principal ports of Southeastern Alaska.

Old and Modern Yakutats

Coming together along the Southeastern coast of Alaska are three Indian races. They are namely the Thlingit, Tsimshean and Haidas. While these races speak different languages they all use a Thlingit jargon for

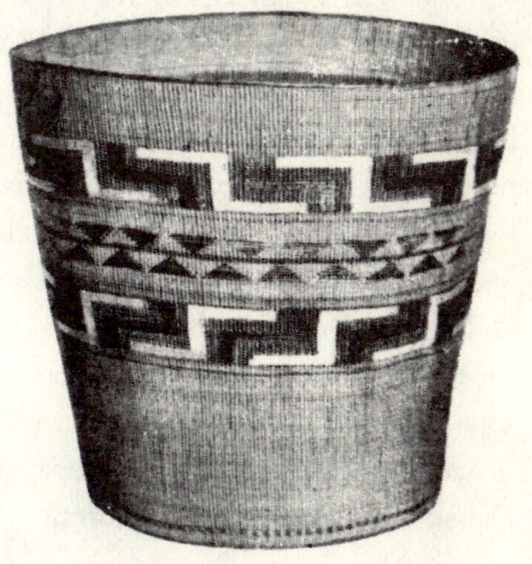

their commerce and trade.   In early days the Thlingits were driven from the Queen Charlotte group of islands by the Haidas and the

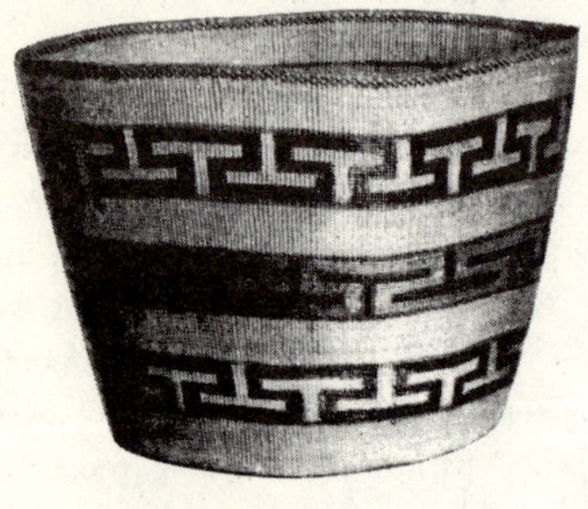

Thlingits now extend from those islands northward along the coast to Prince Williams Sound and penetrate inland on the Stickine and Taku rivers.   The ancient a n d modern Yakutat baskets have been given to the world by this race of people and specimens of the basketry of olden times are eagerly sought for by the tourists.   It now takes a vigorous search of the Indian quarters in the fishing villages to produce any of the old baskets.   Many have been cast away as worn out but the collectors readily seize upon them, paying the natives exorbitant prices for these treasures of a fast dying race.

The early baskets of the Yakutat weavers show considerable ornamentation around the rims and were woven in a solid and substantial manner.   The main texture is spruce roots interwoven with blades of grass and colored with vegetable dyes prepared by a secret process discovered years ago.   This tribe is probably more successful than any other in using to good effect various geometric angles and figures.   The use of such designs has been so constant that the collectors at once recognize a Yakutat basket.   It is said that the use of native dyes among the weavers of the Thlingit tribe is almost a lost art.   They will not return to the old and laborious methods of securing colors when the prepared but inferior dyes can be purchased from northern drug stores.

Preparing the Spruce Roots.

It will of course be interesting to learn how the spruce roots are prepared by the weavers.   The Yakutat Indians obtain these roots from the younger trees, and the task of gathering them falls to the women.   Each root is taken from the ground separately and many are from five to fifteen feet in length.   Root gathering for the manufacture of the pretty and costly baskets is looked upon as an outing for the squaws and the old women often form a party and live for

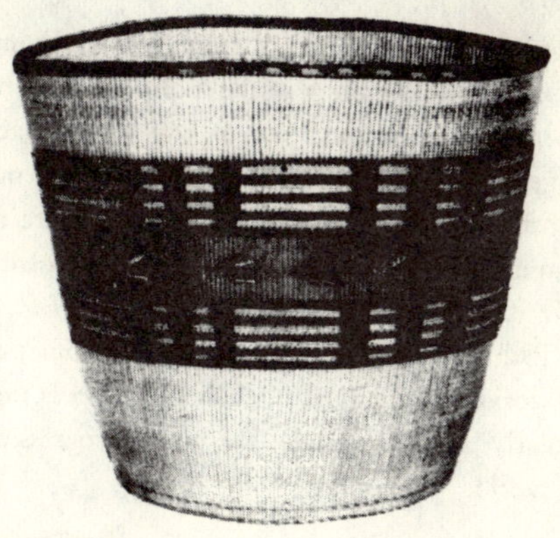

days in the woods collecting a supply that will last them for months After the spruce roots reach the native camp they are first scraped and then parboiled, after which they are placed in pans of water and left for two or three weeks at a time.   When in the judgment of the experienced weaver the roots are finally ready for use they are soaked in a pan of lukewarm water.   The next move on the part of the weaver is to loosen from the root a fibre of desired size.

Many of the ancient Yakutat baskets have seen service as cooking utensils and at the present time there is not probably one to be found in or around the town of Yakutat. Among the Indians in several of the remote villages the collector is most likely to find the handiwork of the early Yakutat weavers. Professor Edmond S. Meany, of the University of Washington, in an article on Alaska Indian basketry, says: "It is not easy to describe the richness and soft beauty of those old baskets, mellowed with time. No one should blame a collector for fondling with ecstacy one of these rare old treasures."

The *Dirigo* and *Farallon* sail from Seattle about every six or seven days, and besides calling at the ports touched by the *Dolphin* and *Jefferson* they go to the "out of the way" places of Alaska. Indian villages, canneries, salteries and mines in the numberless bays and coves of the Islands of Alaska. Travelers who are not particularly in a hurry and want to see Alaska as nearly as possible in its crude and uncivilized state will select the *Dirigo* or *Farallon* for this trip; particularly if they want to see Indians in their homes and get Indian baskets and curios at first hand. The *Farallon* is the only steamer calling regularly at Metlakahtla, the most progressive Indian mission in the world.

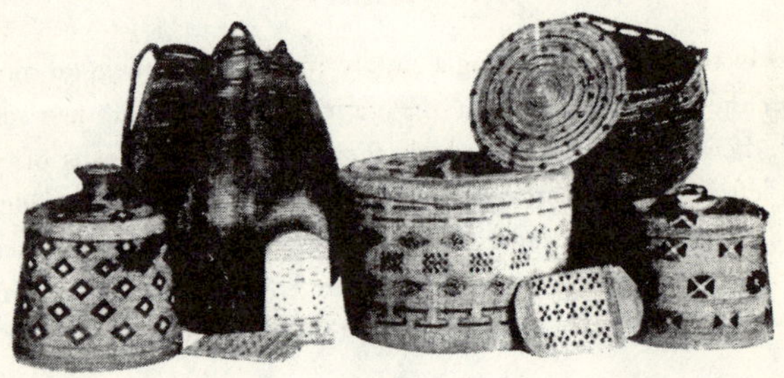

Collecting the Baskets.

Attu and Yakutat baskets may be purchased in any of the northern curio shops. There you will find that the dealers are well up on the subject of Indian basketry and they will be of great assistance to the tourist who is desirous of forming a valuable collection of these rare gems. The baskets are woven in many different shapes. Some are covered, but the majority of those manufactured in Southeastern Alaska are open. The Indian women also make coverings for bottles. High prices do not prevail for the Yakutat basket and they are quoted from $2 to $50. Any of the old weavers know full well the value of their work. If the basket they offer for sale is an inferior one they will always show it in a shame-faced attitude.

During the hot summer days the Indian women and their families display their baskets on the street corners in Skagway, Juneau, Wrangel, Ketchikan, Sitka, Haines and Douglas City. The various curio stores in each of these places carry a full line of baskets and many northern dealers purchase the product of the recognized weavers. Tourists going North should not fail to visit several of the Indian villages on the line of steamship travel. Leaving the

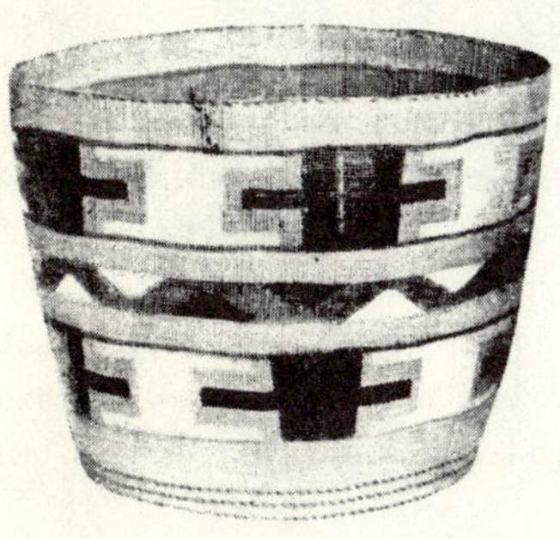

vessel they can roam about from hut to hut conversing with the natives, purchasing the baskets and observing the trophies of the hunt. The handicraft of the native men and women is in evidence everywhere. Besides the Attu and Yakutat baskets those woven by the Fraser river Indians are offered for sale.

Occasionally displays of the Point Barrow basket will be found among the collections of the Alaska dealers.

Like the natives of Attu Island, the Point Barrow Indians use grass in the manufacture of their baskets. They are decorated by the use of reindeer hide and ivory from the tusks of the walrus. The product of the Fraser river Indians is manufactured from the roots of the cedar tree and each basket is ornamented with stripes of wild cherry and crab apple bark in rich browns, reds and yellows. To give variety to the collection the tourist should not fail to procure several baskets woven by the Chilkat Indians. They reside on the

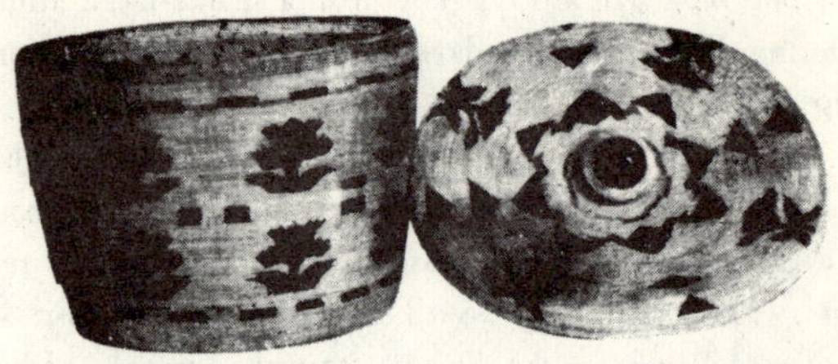

Chilkat river, near Haines Mission, but center about Pyramid Harbor. Their baskets are woven from spruce roots, but little or no coloring is used. The Wrangel Indians make a basket from stripes of cedar bark and weave a few highly-decorated mats. The Haidas also do some weaving and manufacture hats used in their war dances. The tourist upon returning to Seattle from a trip to Southeastern Alaska will be able to complete his collection by adding baskets manufactured by the Indians of Oregon and Washington. Pretty mats can be purchased for a small sum which contribute to the beauty of any basket corner.

Alaska

Alaska is a very much unknown country. The more it is explored and developed the richer it proves. Its extensive and varied resources will employ the talent of our citizens for many years. As its scenic wealth becomes more widely known it will be visited annually by thousands.

Every port at which the steamer stops contains items of great interest to the tourist, and between ports, the long days—sunrise before 3 a. m. and sunset about 10:30 p. m.—give double opportunity to "see." And there are untold and ever-changing wonders to see. Mountains on all sides, glaciers rivalling the famed ones of Switzerland; Indian villages, totem poles, pioneer canneries, etc.

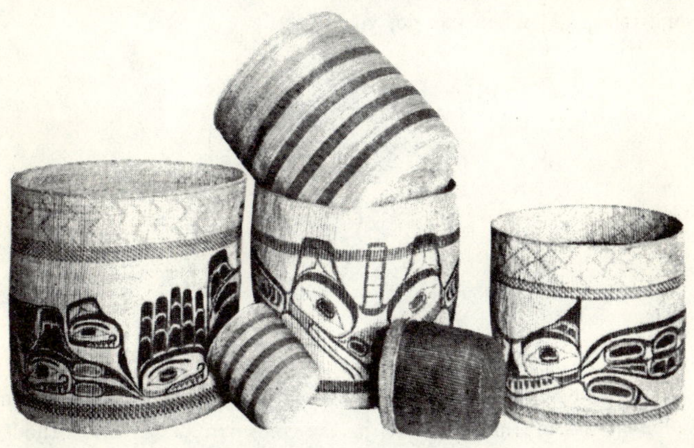

You can lose lots of sleep in a ten-days' trip to Alaska, but you will see more wonderful and beautiful scenery than you can in any other ten-day trip in the world.

You can buy Indian baskets in Seattle and nearly any eastern city, but baskets thus obtained lack the value of those bought from the old Indian woman, in the far off wilds of Alaska. You will prize such acquisitions. Never will you forget that Indian village, with its totem poles and dried fish; its smoky huts and dirty children; its stolid "citizens" and numerous dogs; and the terrible time you had reaching an understanding with the Indian sales lady, and your unsuccessful effort to get a basket or mat at less than the marked price. The basket you bought in Alaska, perhaps at an Indian village in some unfrequented bay on, say, Prince of Wales Island, outvalues a dozen store baskets.

If you think of making a trip to Alaska write us for information and rates, and when you go, go with us.

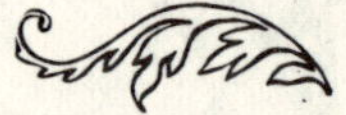

The engravings of baskets contained in this publication are from photographs of Indian baskets in the collection of E. M. Rhodes & Co., 109 Columbia street, Seattle.

A
Catalog Of
SHOREY PUBLICATIONS

1.	Glover, S.L. ORIGIN AND OCCURENCE OF GEM STONES IN WASHINGTON. 1949	1.00
2.	Mooney, Jas. Ghost Dance Religion: SMOHALLA AND HIS DOCTRINE. 1896	1.50
3.	Mooney. Ghost Dance Religion: SHAKERS OF PUGET SOUND. 1896	1.50
5.	DICTIONARY OF CHINOOK JARGON. nd	2.00
6.	ALASKA RAILROAD TIME TABLES. 1922	.50
7.	Wells, E.H. UP AND DOWN THE YUKON. 1900	1.50
8.	Williams, J.G. REPORT OF ATTORNEY GENERAL, Territory of Alaska, 1949-51.	1.50
9.	Gruening, Ernest. MESSAGE OF THE GOVERNOR OF ALASKA, 1946.	2.00
10.	Gruening. THIRD MESSAGE TO THE PEOPLE OF ALASKA, 1946.	1.50
11.	Kohlstedt, E.D. A GLIMPSE OF ALASKA. 1930	1.00
12.	Gruening. MESSAGE OF THE GOVERNOR OF ALASKA, 1945.	2.50
13.	Leehey, M.D. PUBLIC LAND POLICY OF THE U.S. IN ALASKA. 1912	1.50
14.	NOME TELEPHONE DIRECTORY. 1905	3.00
15.	ESTABLISHMENT OF MT. MCKINLEY NATIONAL PARK. 1916	1.50
16.	Hooper, Capt. C.L. CRUISE OF THE U.S. REVENUE STEAMER CORWIN IN ARCTIC OCEAN, November 1, 1880.	7.50
17.	Gruening. MESSAGE TO THE PEOPLE OF ALASKA. 1945	2.00
18.	Gruening. MESSAGES OF THE GOVERNOR OF ALASKA. 1949	2.50
19.	Davis, Geo. T. METLAKAHTLA. 1904	3.50
20.	WORK OF THE BUREAU OF EDUCATION FOR NATIVES OF ALASKA. 1918	5.00
21.	MacDowell, L.W. ALASKA INDIAN BASKETRY.	1.00
22.	Eells, Rev. Myron. THE TWANA, CHEMAKUM & KLALLAM INDIANS OF WASHINGTON TERRITORY. 1887	4.00
23.	Grinnell, Joseph. GOLD HUNTING IN ALASKA.	4.00
24.	Swan, James G. INDIANS OF CAPE FLATTERY.	7.50
25.	CUSTER'S LAST BATTLE. 1892	2.00
26.	Gruening, Sen. INDEPENDENCE DAY ADDRESS. 1959	1.75
27.	Cadell, H.M. THE KLONDIKE AND YUKON GOLDFIELD IN 1913. 1914	2.50
28.	Shiels, Archie W. EARLY VOYAGES OF THE PACIFIC. 1930	3.00
29.	Fickett, E.D. METEOROLOGY. From Explorations in Alaska. 1900	
30.	Richardson, W.P. & others. YUKON RIVER EXPLORING EXPEDITION. Expl. in Alaska. 1900	2.00
31.	Ray, P.H., W.P. Richardson. RELIEF OF THE DESTITUTE IN THE GOLDFIELDS. 1900	1.75
32.	Shiels, Archie W. LITTLE JOURNEYS INTO THE HISTORY OF RUSSIAN AMERICA AND PURCHASE OF ALASKA. 1949	7.50
33.	Shiels. STORY OF TWO DREAMS. 1957	4.00
34.	Swan, J.G. HAIDAH INDIANS OF QUEEN CHARLOTTE'S ISLAND, B.C. 1874	5.00
35.	Butler, Gen. B.V. & the Marquis of Lorne. THE BERING SEA CONTROVERSY. 1892	1.50
36.	Crawford, Lewis F. THE MEDORA-DEADWOOD STAGE LINE. 1925	1.50
37.	Anderson, Eskil. ASBESTOS AND JADE OCCURENCES IN KOBUK RIVER REGION, Alaska. 1945	2.00
38.	Stewart, B.D. PROSPECTING IN ALASKA. 1949	1.50
39.	Geoghegan, Richard H. THE ALEUT LANGUAGE.	5.00
40.	SEATTLE'S FIRST BUSINESS DIRECTORY. 1876	7.50
41.	THE WASHBURN YELLOWSTONE EXPEDITION. 1871	1.25
42.	Subreports from EXPLORATIONS IN ALASKA. 7 reports: The Tanana, Chickaloon, Sushitna, etc. 1900	2.00
43.	Glenn, Capt. E.F. TANANA RIVER EXPLORING EXPEDITION. 1900	2.50
44.	Glenn. COOK'S INLET EXPLORING EXPEDITION. 1900	1.75
45.	WILKESON'S NOTES ON PUGET SOUND (1870?)	2.50
46.	(Perry). JOURNAL OF A VOYAGE TO THE ARCTIC REGIONS IN H.M.S. ALEXANDER, 1818. (1819?)	6.00
47.	BIENNIAL MESSAGE OF WM. M. BUNN, Governor of Idaho. 1884	2.00
48.	MACKENZIE'S ROCK. Exploration of Sir Alexander Mackenzie. 1905	2.50
49.	Williams, L.R. OUR PACIFIC COUNTY (Wash)	5.00
50.	AARON LADNER LINDSLEY..Founder of Alaska Missions.	1.00
51.	Evans, Elwood. PUGET SOUND: Its Past, Present and Future. 1869	2.50
52.	Campbell, Robt. TWO JOURNALS, 1808-1853.	15.00
53.	Bernhardi, Madame Charlotte. MEMOIR OF THE CELEBRATED ADM. JOHN de KRUSENSTERN. 1856	5.00
54.	McWhorter, Lucullus V. CRIME AGAINST THE YAKIMAS. 1931	4.50
55.	Lupton, Chas T. OIL AND GAS IN THE OLYMPIC PENINSULA. 1913	4.00
56.	Seward, Wm. H. THE ADMISSION OF KANSAS. A Speech. 1860	1.50
57.	Stevens, Issac I. PROCLAMATION OF MARTIAL LAW. 1856	.50
58.	THE GLACIER - Tlinkit Training Academy, Vol. II. 1887	.75
59.	Hills, Rev. E.P. REV. AARON L. LINDSLEY.	.50
60.	SWANTON'S HANDBOOK OF NORTH AMERICAN INDIANS, Pt. C: Indians of Alaska & Canada. 1952	5.00
61.	Ward, D.B. ACROSS THE PLAINS IN 1853. 1911	3.50
62.	MacDowell, Lloyd W. ALASKA TOTEM POLES.	1.25
63.	MacDowell. A TRIP TO WONDERFUL ALASKA.	2.00
64.	MacDowell. ALASKA GLACIERS & ICE FIELDS.	1.25
65.	Shaw, Geo. C. THE CHINOOK JARGON AND HOW TO USE IT. 1909	4.00

66.   PUGET SOUND COOPERATIVE COLONY. 1890's   2.00
67.   THE HEROES OF BATTLE ROCK, or The Miners' Reward. 1904   1.50
68.   Lampman, Ben Hur. CENTRALIA TRAGEDY AND TRIAL. 1920   4.00
69.   SEAL FISHERY IN THE NORTH PACIFIC. (Correspondence with Russia.) 1895   7.50
70.   Coolican, J.C. (ed.) PORT ANGELES. 1898   4.00
71.   Jordan, D.S. TROUT AND SALMON OF THE PACIFIC COAST. 1906   1.25
72.   COOPERATIVE PLAN FOR SECURING HOMES AT PORT ANGELES, Wash. 1893   1.00
73.   Hidden, Maria L.T. OREGON PIONEERS. 1910   1.00
74.   Stevens, Hazard. FIRST ASCENT OF TAKHOMA. Ext., 1876   1.50
75.   DEMOCRATIC AND REPUBLICAN Ticket For Washington State and King County. 1889   .50
76.   THIRD ANNUAL COMMENCEMENT OF SEATTLE HIGH SCHOOL. 1888   .35
77.   ASSASSINATION OF PRESIDENT GARFIELD. Newspaper Extra. 1881?   .50
78.   PUGET SOUND CATECHISM. 1889   1.00
79.   SEATTLE, KING COUNTY, WASHINGTON TERRITORY. Statistics & descriptive report.
      1884   1.50
80.   THE GREAT SEATTLE FIRE OF June 6, 1889.   2.50
81.   USGS Bull. 442-D. MINING IN THE CHITINA DIST., etc. 1910   2.50
82.   Swanton, John R. INDIAN TRIBES OF THE PACIFIC NORTHWEST. Ext., 1952   6.00
83.   Sayre, Alex N. PUGET SOUND. Poem 1883   1.50
84.   Bell, W.S. OLD FORT BENTON. 1909   2.50
85.   Meany, Edmund S. INDIAN GEOGRAPHIC NAMES OF WASHINGTON. 1908   1.00
86.   Swanton, J.R. INDIAN TRIBES OF AMERICAN SOUTHWEST. 1952   6.00
87.   Swanton. INDIANS OF MEXICO, CENTRAL AMERICA AND WEST INDIES. 1952   2.50
88.   USGS Bull. 836. SELECTED LIST OF USGS PUBLICATIONS ON ALASKA. 1930   1.00
89.   Lewis, Wm. S. EARLY DAYS IN THE BIG BEND COUNTRY. 1926   3.50
90.   Stoney, Geo. M. EXPLORATIONS IN ALASKA. 1899, Ext. from US Naval Inst.   6.00
91.   Lindsley, A.L. SKETCHES OF AN EXCURSION TO SOUTHERN ALASKA. 1881   5.00
92.   Collins, H.B. ARCHEOLOGY OF THE BERING SEA REGION. Ext., 1933   1.50
93.   Ray and Murdoch. A VOCABULARY OF THE ESKIMOS OF POINT BARROW. 1885   1.25
94.   Andrews, C.L. STORY OF SITKA. 1922   5.00
95.   Matthews, Washington. NAVAJO WEAVERS. 1884   2.50
96.   Dawson, Geo. M. THE HAIDAS. 1882   1.00
97.   McClintock, Walter. FOUR DAYS IN A MEDICINE LODGE. 1900   1.00
98.   Barbeau, Marius. MODERN GROWTH OF THE TOTEM POLES ON THE NORTHWEST COAST.
      1939   1.00
99.   SCRIPTURE SELECTIONS AND HYMNS IN HIDATSA or GROS VENTURE LANGUAGE. 1906   1.50
100. Baker, Marcus. GEOGRAPHIC DICTIONARY OF ALASKA. 1906   3.00
101. Lee, Charles A. ALEUTIAN INDIAN AND ENGLISH DICTIONARY. 1896   1.00
102. Shaw, Geo. C. VANCOUVER'S DISCOVERY OF PUGET SOUND IN 1792. 1933   1.00
103. Seward, Wm. H. SPEECHES in Alaska, Vancouver, and Oregon, 1869.   2.50
104. Rees, J.E. IDAHO: Chronology, Nomenclature, Biblio. 1918   5.00
105. Smith, W.C. THE EVERETT MASSACRE. 1916   8.00
106. PLACER MINING. 1897   4.50
107. Ross, Clyde P. THE VALDEZ CREEK MINING DISTRICT IN ALASKA. 1933   5.00
108. Stevens, Isaac I. TREATY BETWEEN THE U.S. AND THE DWAMISH, SUQUAMISH, & OTHER
      ALLIED AND SUBORDINATE TRIBES OF INDIANS IN WASHINGTON TERRITORY. 1855   2.00
109. Stevens, I.I. TREATY BETWEEN THE U.S. & THE NISQUALLY & OTHER BANDS OF INDIANS.
      1855   2.00
110. Stevens. TREATY BETWEEN THE U.S. & THE YAKIMA NATION OF INDIANS. 1855   2.00
111. Stevens. TREATY BETWEEN THE U.S. OF A. & THE MAKAH TRIBE OF INDIANS. 1855   2.00
112. Stevens. TREATY BETWEEN THE U.S. AND THE INDIANS OF THE WILLAMETTE VALLEY.
      1855   2.00
113. Densmore, F. STUDY OF INDIAN MUSIC. 1941   1.50
114. Harriman, Job. THE CLASS WAR IN IDAHO.   3.00
115. Ranck, G. PICTURES FROM NORTHWEST HISTORY.   2.00
116. Whitaker, R. OVERLAND TO OREGON. 1906   4.00
117. Krieger, H. INDIAN VILLAGES OF S.E. ALASKA.   2.50
118. Gatschet, A. THE KLAMATH INDIANS OF SOUTHWEST OREGON. 1890   4.50
119. Crane, W. TOTEM TALES. 1952   4.00
120. Bate, J. THE SECOND BOOKE TEACHING MOST PLAINLY AND COMPOSING OF ALL MANNER
      OF FIREWORKS FOR TRYUMPH AND RECREATION. 1635   3.00
121. James, G. PRACTICAL BASKET MAKING. 1917   5.00
122. Whorf, B. MAYA HIEROGLYPHS. 1941   1.25
123. Dall, Wm. MASKS, LABRETS, AND CERTAIN ABORIGINAL CUSTOMS. 1884   8.50
124. McCurdy, J. CAPE FLATTERY AND ITS LIGHT.   1.00
125. Wilhelm, Homer. THE SAN JUAN ISLANDS. 1901   5.00
126. Gaerity, Jack. BREAD AND ROSES FROM STONE.   4.00
127. Smith, W.C. WAS IT MURDER? (Centralia) 1922   3.50
128. HISTORY OF OWYHEE COUNTY. (Idaho)   8.50
129. Evans, Elwood. WASHINGTON TERRITORY. 1877   3.00
130. Delaney, Matilda Sagar. THE WHITMAN MASSACRE. 1920   3.00
131. Hubback, T.W. TEN THOUSAND MILES TO ALASKA FOR MOOSE AND SHEEP. 1921   4.00
132. Wilson, Katherine. COPPER-TINTS. 1923   3.00
133. Coleman, Edmund T. FIRST ASCENT OF MT. BAKER. Ext. from Harper's Monthly.
      1869   2.50
134. Hodge, L.K. (ed.) MINING IN THE PACIFIC NORTHWEST. 1897   30.00
134a. Hodge. MINING IN WESTERN WASHINGTON. Ext from #134   10.00

134b. Hodge. MINING IN CENTRAL & EASTERN WASHINGTON. Ext. from #134   10.00
134c. Hodge. MINING IN SOUTHERN BRITISH COLUMBIA. Ext. from #134   10.00
135. Stallard, Bruce. ARCHEOLOGY IN WASHINGTON. 1958   3.00
136. Lockley, Fred. ALASKA'S FIRST FREE MAIL DELIVERY IN 1900.   1.25
137. Strange. JAMES STRANGE'S JOURNAL AND NARRATIVE OF THE COMMERCIAL EXPEDITION
      FROM BOMBAY TO THE NORTHWEST COAST OF AMERICA. 1928   5.00
138. Hathaway, Ella C. BATTLE OF THE BIG HOLE.   2.00
139. Haller, Granville. SAN JUAN & SECESSION.   1.50
140. THE KLONDIKE NEWS. Vol. 1 #1, Dawson Newspaper. 1898 (Alaska's rarest
      newspaper)   10.00
141. JOURNAL OF MEDOREM CRAWFORD. 1897   2.00
142. OCOSTA! The Ocean Terminus of the Northern Pacific R.R. and Coast City of
      Washington.   2.50
143. Sutherland, T.A. HOWARD'S CAMPAIGN AGAINST THE NEZ PERCE INDIANS, 1877.
      1878   3.50
144. Matthews, Mathew. THE CATLIN COLLECTION OF INDIAN PAINTINGS. 1890   3.00
145. Lockley, Fred. TO OREGON BY OX TEAM IN '47.   1.25
146. Lockley. VIGILANTE DAYS IN VIRGINIA CITY.   1.50
147. Judson, Katherine. MYTHS AND LEGENDS OF THE PACIFIC NORTHWEST. 1910   7.50
148. Whiting, Dr. F.B. GRIT, GRIEF AND GOLD.   10.00
149. Amundsen, Capt. Roald. TO THE NORTH MAGNETIC POLE AND THROUGH THE NORTHWEST
      PASSAGE.   3.00
150. Butte Businessmen's Assn. BUTTE, MONTANA.   2.00
151. Immigration Aid Society of Washington Terr. NORTHWESTERN WASHINGTON. 1880   3.50
152. Denig, Edwin T. INDIAN TRIBES OF THE UPPER MISSOURI. 1930   10.00
153. Buckley, Rev. J.M. TWO WEEKS IN THE YOSEMITE AND VICINITY. 1888   2.50
154. SPEECH OF THE HON. R.C. WINTHROP OF MASS. ON THE PRESIDENT'S MESSAGE (on
      admission of California) 1850   2.00
155. Marshall, Martha. A PRONOUNCING DICTIONARY OF CALIFORNIA NAMES IN ENGLISH
      AND SPANISH.   2.50
156. Mercer, A.S. BIG HORN COUNTY, WYOMING.   7.50
157. Moorehead, Warren K. PREHISTORIC RELICS.   7.50
158. Merrill, Geo. P. NOTES ON THE GEOLOGY AND NATURAL HISTORY OF THE PENIN-
      SULA OF LOWER CALIFORNIA. 1895   2.00
159. Georgeson, C.C. REINDEER & CARIBOU. 1904   1.50
160. Hewett, Edgar L. A GENERAL VIEW OF THE ARCHEOLOGY OF THE PUEBLO REGION.
      1904   2.00
161. Bennett, Wm. P. THE FIRST BABY IN CAMP.   3.50
162. Coffman, Noah B. OLD LEWIS COUNTY, Oregon Territory. 1926   3.50
163. Bebbe, Mrs. Iola. THE TRUE LIFE STORY OF SWIFTWATER BILL GATES. 1908   7.50
164. Costello. THE SIWASH - THEIR LIFE, LEGENDS AND TALES. 1895   10.00
165. Murie, Olaus J. ALASKA-YUKON CARIBOU.   10.00
166. Meeker, Ezra. STORY OF THE LOST TRAIL TO OREGON, NO. 2. 1916   2.50
167. Hanna, Rev. J.A. DR. WHITMAN AND HIS RIDE TO SAVE OREGON. 1903   1.25
168. Hadwen, Seymore & Laurence J. Palmer. REINDEER IN ALASKA. 1922   5.00
169. Geer, T.T. THE ROMANCE OF ASTORIA. 1911   1.75
170. Williams, Lewis. CHINOOK BY THE SEA.   7.50
171. SAN FERNANDO VALLEY. 1938   2.00
172. PASADENA. 1938   2.00
173. Ingalls, Maj. J.W. HISTORY OF WASHOE COUNTY, NEVADA. 1913   5.00
174. Reid, J.T. & J.R. Hunter. HUMBOLT COUNTY. 1913   4.50
175. Aston. ESMERALDA COUNTY. 1913   4.50
176. London, Jack. THE GOLD HUNTERS OF THE NORTH. Ext., 1903.   1.25
177. Wartman-Arland, Flora E. THE STORY OF MONTESANO. 1933   4.00
178. London. THE ECONOMICS OF THE KLONDIKE.   1.50
179. Bishop, Robert Sr. LAND IN THE SKY TOTEM.   1.50
180. Webb, John S. & Ed S. Curtis. THE RIVER TRIP TO THE KLONDIKE AND THE RUSH
      TO THE KLONDIKE OVER THE MOUNTAIN PASS. 1898   2.50
181. Librn. of Bellingham Public Libr. HISTORY OF BELLINGHAM. 1926   6.00
182. VOYAGE OF ALEXANDER MACKENZIE.   2.50
183. Chaplin, Ralph. CENTRALIA CONSPIRACY.   4.50
184. Haswell, Robert. ROBERT HASWELL'S JOURNALS. 1788-89.   4.00
185. Minto, John. RHYME OF EARLY LIFE IN OREGON. (1915?)   4.00
186. Collins, Henry B., A.H. Clarke & E.H. Walker. THE ALEUTIAN ISLANDS: Their
      People & Natural History. 1945   7.50
187. Simpson, Brevet Brig. Gen. J.H. CORONADO'S MARCH IN SEARCH OF THE "SEVEN
      CITIES OF CIBOLA." 1871   2.50
188. Riddle, Geo. W. EARLY DAYS IN OREGON.   5.00
189. VILHJALMUR STEFANSON. 1925   2.50
190. Lockley, Fred. ACROSS THE PLAINS BY PRAIRIE SCHOONER.   1.50
191. MacArthur, Walter. LAST DAYS OF SAIL ON THE WEST COAST. 1929   7.50
192. Stuck, Hudson. T E ALASKAN MISSIONS OF THE EPISCOPAL CHURCH. 1920   10.00
193. Steffa, Don. TALES OF NOTED FRONTIER CHARACTERS, SOAPY SMITH. 1908   1.75.
194. Meeker, E. WASGUBGTIB TERRUTIRT, k870   3.00
195. Denny, Arthur A. PIONEER DAYS ON PUGET SOUND. 1888   5.00
196. Rowan, James. THE I.W.W. IN THE LUMBER INDUSTRY.   4.00
199. Sayre, J. Willis. THE EARLY WATERFRONT OF SEATTLE, 1937.   2.50

204. Pelly, T.M.   DR. MINOR - A SKEtch of His Background and Life. 1933   7.50
209. Flandrau, Grace. FRONTIER DAYS ALONG THE UPPER MISSOURI.   3.00
210. Flandrau. THE LEWIS AND CLARK EXPEDITION.   5.00
211. Flandrau. A GLANCE AT THE LEWIS AND CLARK EXPEDITION.   3.00
213. Flandrau. THE VERENDRYE OVERLAND QUEST OF THE PACIFIC.   3.50
216. Harper, Frank B. FORT UNION AND ITS NEIGHBORS ON THE UPPER MISSOURI.   2.50
220. Burdick, Usher L. MARQUIS de MORES AT WAR IN THE BADLANDS. 1929   2.50
227. General Strike Committee. THE SEATTLE GENERAL STRIKE. 1919   5.00
231. Sayre, J.W. THE ROMANCE OF SECOND AVENUE.   1.50
235. DEDICATION AND OPENING OF THE NEW CASCADE TUNNEL. 1929   2.00
239. Van Olinda, O.S. HISTORY OF VASHON - MAURY ISLAND. 1935   6.00
241. Hanford, C.H. SAN JUAN DISPUTE. 1900   2.00
246. Walgamott, C.S. REMINISCENCES OF EARLY DAYS. 1926   7.50
250. Wardner, Jim. JIM WARDNER, OF WARDNER IDAHO. 1900   8.00
251. Brown, Col. W.C. THE SHEEPEATER CAMPAIGN, Idaho - 1879. 1926   2.50
259. Hornaday, Wm. T. EXTERMINATION OF THE AMERICAN BISON. 1887?   10.00
264. Slauson, Morda C. ONE HUNDRED YEARS ON THE CEDAR.   10.00
265. Jones, S.C. & M.F. Casady. FROM CABIN TO CUPOLA. County Courthouses in
          Washington.   10.00
267. Andrews, Clarence L. WRANGELL AND THE GOLD OF THE CASSIAR. 1937   3.50
268. Andrews, Clarence L. THE PIONEERS AND THE NUGGETS OF VERSE. 1937   3.00
280. PORT TOWNSEND. 1890   5.00
281. Gilbert, Kenneth. ALASKAN POKER STORIES. 1958   2.50
282. Moore, James Bernard. SKAGWAY IN DAYS PRIMEVAL.   4.00
283. Chase, Cora G. UNTO THE LEAST. 1972   6.00
284. Blankenship, Geo. E. EARLY HISTORY OF THURSTON COUNTY. 1914   20.00
285. Fish, Harriet U. PAST AT PRESENT. 1967   12.50
286. Allen, Edward W. THE ROLLICKING PACIFIC; A Selection of Poems. 1972   3.00
287. Allen. DANCING TALES. 1951   4.00

SJU 1.   Farlow, Dr. W.G. SOME EDIBLE AND POISONOUS FUNGI. 1897   2.50
SJU 2.   Gurdji, V. ORIENTAL RUG WEAVING. 1901   5.00
SJU 3.   D'Avenes, E., Prisse & Dr. J.C. Ewart. EGYPTIAN AND ARABIAN HORSES AND
          ORIGIN OF HORSES AND PONIES. 1904   2.50
SJU 4.   Freshfield, Douglas W. ON MOUNTAINS AND MANKIND. 1904   1.50
SJU 5.   Davenport, Cyril. CAMEOS. 1904   1.50
SJU 6.   Maire, Albert. MATERIALS USED TO WRITE UPON BEFORE THE INVENTION OF
          PRINTING.   1.50
SJU 7.   Liberty, Arthur L. PEWTER AND THE REVIVAL OF ITS USE. 1904   1.50
SJU 8.   Hammell, Wm. PINE NEEDLE BASKETRY.   1.50
SJU 9.   Frey, Clark, Vietch. HOME TANNING. 1936   1.50
SJU 10.   Browning, Frank. STEAM PLANT ERRORS   2.00
SJU 18.   Burdick, Arthur J. THE PROSPECTOR'S MANUAL. 1905   7.50
SJU 19.   WOODS DUAL POWER. (1902?)   1.50
SJU 20.   Hayward, Charles B. DIRIGIBLE BALLOONS. 1921   5.00
SJU 21.   Osborn, Henry F. THE ELEPHANTS AND MASTEDONS ARRIVE IN AMERICA   1.50
SJU 22.   Todd, Mattie Phipps. HAND LOOM WEAVING. 1902   7.00
SJU 23.   Wilbur, C. Martin. HISTORY OF THE CROSSBOW. 1936   1.50
SJU 24.   Alexander, A.S. HORSE SECRETS. 1913   2.50
SJU 26.   Clute, Willard Nelson. THE FERN - COLLECTOR'S GUIDE. 1901   3.00
SJU 27.   Meeker, E. HOP CULTURE IN THE U.S. 1883   10.00

SJI 1.   Krause, F. SLING CONTRIVANCES. 1904   2.00
SJI 2.   Murdoch, John. A STUDY OF THE ESKIMO BOWS IN THE U.S. NATIONAL MUSEUM.   1.50
          1884
SJI 3.   Mason, Otis T. THROWING STICKS IN THE NATIONAL MUSEUM. 1884.   2.50
SJI 4.   CHIEF JOSEPH'S OWN STORY. 1879   2.50
SJI 5.   Mason, Otis. BASKET WORK OF THE ABORIGINES. 1884   5.00
SJI 6.   Llwd, Rev. Dr. J.P.D. THE MESSAGE OF AN INDIAN RELIC: Seattle's Totem
          Pole.   2.00
SJI 7.   Mason, O. TRAPS OF THE AMERICAN INDIAN.   1.25
SJI 8.   Meeker, Louis L. OGALALA GAMES. 1901   1.50
SJI 9.   Collins, Henry B. PREHISTORIC ART OF THE ALASKAN ESKIMO. 1929   3.50
SJI 10.   Eells, Rev. M. JUSTICE TO THE INDIAN.   1.00
SJI 11.   Willoughby, C. INDIANS OF THE QUINAIELT AGENCY, Washington Territory.
          1886   1.50
SJI 12.   Leon & Holmes. STUDIES ON THE ARCHAEOLOGY OF MICHOACAN MEXICO... 1886   2.00
SJI 13.   Beckwith, Paul. NOTES ON CUSTOMS OF THE DAKOTAHS. 1886   1.25
SJI 14.   Eells, Rev. M. THE STONE AGE. 1886   1.50
SJI 15.   Allen, Lt. Henry T. ATNATANAS NATIVES OF COPPER RIVER, ALASKA. 1886   1.00
SJI 16.   Yates, Dr. L.G. CHARM STONES. 1886   1.50
SJI 17.   Boas, Fran . THE CENTRAL ESKIMO. 1884   12.50
SJI 18.   Gibbs, Geo. & others. TRIBES OF THE EXTREME NORTHWEST, ALASKA, THE
          ALEUTIANS AND ADJACENT TERRITORIES. Ext. 1877   15.00
SJI 19.   Gibbs & others. LANGUAGES OF THE TRIBES OF THE EXTREME NORTHWEST, ALASKA,
          THE ALEUTIANS AND ADJACENT TERRITORY.   6.00

SJI 20. Gibbs, Geo., Dr. Wm. F. Tolmie, & Father G. Mengarini. TRIBES OF
         WESTERN WASHINGTON AND NORTHWESTERN OREGON.   20.00
SJI 21. Gibbs, Geo & others. COMPARATIVE VOCABULARIES OF THE TRIBES OF WESTERN
         WASHINGTON AND NORTHWESTERN OREGON. part of SJI 20.   5.00
SJI 22. Gibbs, Geo. A DICTIONARY OF THE NISQUALLY INDIAN LANGUAGE. part of
         SJI 20.   10.00
SJI 23. Boas, Franz. INTRODUCTION TO HANDBOOK OF AMERICAN INDIAN LANGUAGES. Ext.
         1911   5.00
SJI 24. Swanton, John R. THE TLINGIT INDIAN LANGUAGE. From Hndbk. of Amer.
         Indian Lang.   3.00
SJI 25. Swanton. THE HAIDA INDIAN LANGUAGE.   5.00
SJI 26. Boas. THE TSIMSHIAN INDIAN LANGUAGE.   8.00
SJI 27. Boas. THE KWAKIUTL INDIAN LANGUAGE.   7.50
SJI 28. Boas. THE CHINOOK INDIAN LANGUAGE.   5.00
SJI 29. Boas & Swanton. THE SIOUAN, Dakota INDIAN LANGUAGE.   6.00
SJI 30. Talbitzer, Wm. THE ESKIMO LANGUAGE.   6.50
SJI 31. Ewers, John C. EARLY WHITE INFLUENCE UPON PLAINS INDIAN PAINTING. 1957   2.00
SJI 32. Fenton, Wm. N. CONTRACTS BETWEEN IROQUOIS HERBALISM AND COLONIAL MEDICINE.
         1941   2.00
SJI 38. Remington, Fred. ARTIST WANDERINGS AMONG THE CHEYENNES. 1889   1.50
SJI 41. Bagley, Clarence. INDIAN MYTHS OF THE NORTHWEST. 1930   8.50
SJI 43. Mason, O. ABORIGINAL SKIN DRESSING.   5.00
SJI 46. Thorne, J. Frederic. IN THE TIME THAT WAS. 1909   2.50
SJI 49. DeSmet, Rev. P.J. NEW INDIAN SKETCHES.   8.50
SJI 51. Mason, O. MAN'S KNIFE AMONG THE NORTH AMERICAN INDIANS. 1899   2.00
SJI 53. Holmes, William H. POTTERY OF THE ANCIENT PUEBLOS. 1886   6.00
SJI 55. Dorsey, James O. A STUDY OF SIOUAN CULTS   1894   10.00
SJI 57. Mason, O. POINTED BARK CANOES OF THE KUTENAI AND AMUR. 1901   2.00
SJI 58. Mason, O. ABORIGINAL AMERICAN HARPOONS. 1902   7.50
SJI 59. Hough, Walter. THE LAMP OF THE ESKIMO. 1898   5.00
SJI 61. Drucker, Philip. ARCHAEOLOGICAL SURVEY ON THE NORTHERN NORTHWEST COAST.
         1943.   7.00
SJI 62. INDIANS IN WASHINGTON.   3.00

<u>NOTE TO STUDENTS AND COLLECTORS</u>

    Many scarce items turn up in antiquarian book stores only once. And while such
works are in great demand, the high prices usually commanded by the older, scarcer
items put them beyond the reach of the average student and the small collector. To
meet this need we are bringing back into print a diversity of Pacific Northwest and
Alaskan historical material which we are selling at moderate prices. In their original form these bring prices ranging from $3.00 to $100.00; some even higher.

    We limit most   reproductions from 25 to 100 copies and reprint as the demand
warrants. The books have heavy paper covers. They show both original and reprinting
dates. Regular library and dealer discounts granted. For detailed descriptions of
these titles send for Shorey's Catalog of Publications #3. It also lists future
Shorey Publications.